Andrew Graves is a freelance writer and poet. His last two collections, *Light at the end of the Tenner* and *God Save the Teen* were released through Burning Eye Books. His first non-fiction title *Welcome to the Cheap Seats: Silver Screen Portrayals of the British Working Class*, was published by Five Leaves Books in 2018 and his next book, an analysis of Alice Lowe's film *Prevenge* will be published by Auteur Publishing very shortly. He is currently writing a book about *A Field in England* for Electric Dreamhouse. He is host of Mondo Moviehouse: The Weird World Cinema podcast and is a regular contributor to Scream Magazine, Diabolique, The Digital Fix, Arrow Films, 88 Films, BFI , Eureka, Second Sight and We Belong Dead.

Not Dancing
with Ingrid Pitt

Andrew Graves

Burning Eye

BurningEyeBooks
Never Knowingly
Mainstream

Copyright © 2021 Andrew Graves

The author asserts the moral right under the Copyright, Designs and Patents Act 1988 to be identified as the author of this work.

All rights reserved. No part of this publication may be reproduced, stored in a retrieval system, or transmitted, in any form or by any means without the prior written consent of the author, nor be otherwise circulated in any form of binding or cover other than that in which it is published and without a similar condition being imposed on the subsequent purchaser.

This edition published by Burning Eye Books 2021

www.burningeye.co.uk

@burningeyebooks

Burning Eye Books
15 West Hill, Portishead, BS20 6LG

ISBN 978-1-911570-88-2

Not Dancing with Ingrid Pitt

for Anna, Siouxsie and Lily

CONTENTS

NEON CHIP SHOP SMILES
Electric	12
Nylon Flights of Fancy	13
Bathroom Tabs	14
Sidekick	15
Still Notts Talking	16
Scarborough	17
This Town	18
Gentlemen's Excuse Me	21

PINK ANGORA TRASH CAN LOVE
Not Dancing with Ingrid Pitt	24
Distance Travelled	26
Golden Turkey Testament	28
Marilyn	30
November 1st	31
Finding Myself	32
Google Search Inspired Poem #1	33

SUPERKING-TAINTED WISDOM
Network	36
Packing	37
Waiting	38
Potholes and Parking	41
The Futurist Cinema	42
Comic Timing	43
You Are Every Everything, I Am Every Nothing	44
What Is Your Music?	45
No Socialist Grace	48

THIS AND THAT

Home Front	50
Tea Poem	51
Phone	52
February 14th	54
Poor Sunday	55
Street Dance	56
Getting Lost	57
This and That	60
Moviedrome	61
Perfectly Damaged	62
Paz	63
Dreamin'	65

NEON CHIP SHOP SMILES

ELECTRIC

I saw them.
Haunting the north bay promenade,
a waking flush in the stillborn dark.

He, a phantom Captain Blythe,
threatened by a mutiny of rains;
she, a Bride of Frankenstein,
Mary Shelley, magic muse,
cast in shockwave deco-perm.

They held hands
by the harboured boats
that bobbed and rocked on
a black glass sea,
its infinity broke by red, green shimmers,
reflecting neon chip shop smiles.

They kissed by the rotting Futurist,
poor relative to Whitby's vampire ruin,
a posthumous, parting lightning snog,
lips, a static ghost machine.

They glowed as arcade cinema gods, their love ablaze on the closed-up pier,

shaming the slithering, half-lost moon, a mad dream's spark,

a cold dead night.

NYLON FLIGHTS OF FANCY

When me and our Martyn were boys
Mam gave us butterfly catchers
fashioned out of garden canes,
hoops of wire and the legs of old American tan tights.

They became our favourite summertime tools,
homemade dream snatchers.
Together we swept the neighbour's heaving buddleia,
excitedly laddering the sky
with our little nets of joy
that fluttered with proud childishness
and dancing powder-blushed
captured wings.

BATHROOM TABS

In her last years, Grandma
used to live in a flat with her son, my uncle.

He didn't like her smoking inside,
but she loved to cane the fags.
As a compromise, she agreed
to only smoke in the bathroom.

I smoked at that time too,
but, being on the dole and always skint,
I'd often follow her in there to blag a quick tab.

She never let me down.
We'd talk about nothing and everything,
on a level not found in other smokeless rooms.

Eventually I quit
and Grandma died not long back.
I've never really missed the ciggies,
definitely not the cost,
but I do miss that creaky knackered bathtub
with an old lady perched upon it,
casting her ash into the sink
and Superking-tainted wisdom
to a lost and penniless,
gormless grandson.

SIDEKICK

As a kid, I was never into sport.
Batman was my footy.
A parka worn as cape around
the neck was my kit,
the dynamic duo my team,
Adam West
my Georgie Best.

STILL NOTTS TALKING

It's an accent left out in the rain,
huddled at the doorway
to nowhere special,
hood pulled tight around its face,
feeling the *cowd*, not the cold.

It's a distant bedraggled cousin
of Northernness,
not scouse, not Yorkshire,
Brummie or Manc;
it's the one you can't quite do,
can't quite figure out.

It's an echoing drawn-out
slang of the heart,
with its slab square yammer
and sarky comments,
ripping through the rubbish and rammel.

It tugs no forelocks,
doffs no caps;
it'll take you
down a peg or two

where men still
call each other *duck*.

It's served with chips and batter bits,
oiled with Raleigh factory grease,
choked with seventies slagheap dust;

it'll sugar the tea,
warm the plates

and give its seat up on the bus.

SCARBOROUGH

It's a proper Scarborough evening sky,
a neon lilac sci-fi glow.
A last dance at the season's end,
amusements and the sea in awe
of God's electric boogaloo.

THIS TOWN

In this town, an unexpected
February sun is a gate-crashed light
on the bookie's shop.
Not so much the promise
of spring as a quickly scribbled IOU.

This town has weathered its share of rain, had its lotto card scratched
and chucked in the bin, has lapsed
into afternoons of avenues and joining the backs
of endless queues.

This town is the old picture house
now turned into a bingo hall,
where the movie is always Ken Loach, kitchen-sink suggestive,
viewed with middle-class suspicion reduced to Channel 5 clichés,
vape shop, casino,
car-crash telly.

In this town, the one pub that remains open
burns majestic,
a carnival star;
it makes an extra show of itself
in the absence of dark and closed-up cousins,
a hopeful ace in a rubbish hand.

This town is the miner, thirty years forgotten,
still blinking in the light of progress undelivered.
It's the last of the union,
singing against the stinging of cold
dead machines, hymns, not for *X Factor*
but for ex-factories.

This town has seen too much,
legs knocked from under it,
kicked in the teeth, the place
where liberal heart fingers

will not reach.

This town.

But this town is the road.
It's the brick, the stone and
the soul.

It's the grit and the spit,
the need to go on.

It's the little girl protected from
all this, by her mam and dad's resistance
and a goodnight kiss.

It's the guts and the glory
and it is its own story.
This town will form its own narrative,
be the hero, not the zero-
contract-hours statistic.

Will refuse to be a shadow in the foodbank line.
Will be no one's stock character,
no one's *Guardian* piece or thing to be pitied.

This town can be its own allotment,
where the germination of ideas
will form gardens of prosperity.

Where growing up won't mean
waiting around to be pushed back down.

This town can form its own community.
Forge new attitudes.
Mend all the torn histories.
Mine for different futures.

This town can be its own industry,
manufacturing possibilities

on conveyor belts of truth.

This town, this town.

Still working towards its promise of spring.

GENTLEMEN'S EXCUSE ME

They sit by the window in that caravan,
silhouettes framed by Skeggy sun
as it sneaks behind the fairground rides,
distant flickering neon stars at play amidst the smoking dusk.

And she leans against him,
drunkenly falling awkward into sunburnt arms,
and between cider kisses
sparkling onto busy lips

someone on the telly says,

If you stay with me I'll dance all my dances with you.

And maybe it's the drink,
but he thinks that's
the best line he's ever heard

and in that second
he'd gladly choreograph
an eternity with her.

But she just laughs,
says it's corny,

reminds him that he's no John Travolta,
he'll never be on *Strictly*.

They kiss again,
and again,

then shimmy into forever
or however long the
weekend lasts.

PINK ANGORA
TRASH CAN LOVE

NOT DANCING WITH INGRID PITT

for Ingrid Pitt (1937–2010)

I was so close we could have touched, held hands, danced.
I must have walked past her a million times before,
and I was doing it again.

I'd catch her the next time,
I said to myself,
she being a regular face on the convention trail,
with her autograph-swirling Sharpie
scribbling spells
across sweaty-pawed posters
of *The Vampire Lovers*.

I was young. She wasn't,
a slight tremble in those
liver-spot creping,
Hammer Horror hands.

But those eyes. Christ, those eyes.
Piercing, Polish, perfect.
Those eyes were
Countess Dracula,
Wicker Man Medusa,
blazing heretic beacons,
Carpathian crystal magic pools.

And still I never stopped.

At the end of the show
I watched her pack away publicity stills,
walk away from spotlit auditorium,

the longest shadow in the NEC.

She never came back.

And I wished we'd touched,
held hands,
danced.

Instead I was left
with a memory,
an unplayed song,
a Mephisto Waltz
and a stake through
idiot fanboy heart.

DISTANCE TRAVELLED

He dons khaki shorts, even though it's December.
They expose blotchy
pink, frost-cracked skin.

He looks about for a place on the bus
through NHS specs that
retain only one lens, a sticking plaster
holding the plastic bridge together
but not his self-possession.

Everyone hopes he won't choose
the seat next to them.
Bags suddenly appear from nowhere,
knees splay out erratically,
creating the illusion of no more space.
There's no room here,
a million silent screams cry out.
Each pair of eyes searches
desperately for places not to look.

He chooses the seat next to me.
He smiles.
I smile.
It seems the only option. Besides, he has
one of those photofit faces,
a look that I can imagine staring
back at me from the pages of
Murder Casebook.

Inevitably, he begins the conversation
which only one of us wants to happen.

He tells me that most twopences
are worth less than two pence.
That *they* can cure blindness
with a photocopier.
That pyramids are really spaceships,

that Hitler is in a deep freeze unit
underneath the White House
and that the fabric of reality is about to unravel,

and, more quietly, that his mum is still unwell.

Eventually, he reaches his stop and I am
relieved when he goes.

And when he gets off the bus by the hospice

I suspect that the fabric of reality isn't the only thing
about to come apart.

And I hope I see him on the trip back,

where this time I'll be happy to be part
of his shadowy conspiracy
if only for half an hour,

be his dark passenger
on a journey which is
bound to crash and
no doubt be covered
up by the CIA.

GOLDEN TURKEY TESTAMENT

for Ed Wood (1924–1978), 'Worst Director of All Time'

Oh, Eddie, be vodka make-believe,
save us from our clarity,
be a clapperboard-slapping chaos lost
in the boulevards of the bad.

Be a relic, redundant, ridiculed,
reduced and reclusive,
a gatecrashed Hollywood
monochrome ghost,
flickering,
oblivious.

Be a fog-bound bottomless
reeking swamp,
a twisting forest, dementia-dark,
a distant crumbling castle lab
of Lugosi-stalking junkie hell.

Be a Halloween midnight
drive-in crash,
a corset-laced-up funeral,
a vampire girl
or wrestling dude
stumbling
into cardboard tombs.

Be terrible theremin sci-fi squeals,
a crossdressed choir boy
horror-flick hymn;
be a slavering gentle genius
dancing the bug-eyed boogaloo.

Be radioactive,
wrecked, a victim,
an experiment spooled
from poverty row,
a distant, disquieted ragtag freak
of pink angora trash can love.

MARILYN

You were gone.
Not just gone but Hollywood gone.
Like you'd always never really been there.

Lookalike. Box set. Poster.
The pin-up girl we tried to pin down in a newsreel kiss,
a lipstick curse miscarrying into childless ache
when *Some Like It Hot* ran cold.

Barbiturate bombshell blown to smithereens,
peroxide pieces scattered at a playground's edge.

You were star and rumour,
shimmer and shadow,
skirt and steam,
dirt and dream,

magic, misfit,
Norma Jeane.

NOVEMBER 1ST

Fishnets slither over unmade sheets,
black abandoned devil snakes snagged by eager vampire claws
in a trick-or-treating kind of love;
its spell broke in November's dawn.

Now, dust motes in the murky light
dance like funeral home confetti to settle on a pumpkin carved
with guilty morning-after smile,
fag nubs shoved through orange teeth.

And spiders crawl across her eyes,
a mascara-bleeding waking gaze
that sees him struggling into jeans
and fastening up his joke-shop cape.

No red lips pressed to zombie's cheek.

No number left, no words exchanged.

Embarrassed, she feigns an undead sleep
whilst Dracula does the walk of shame.

FINDING MYSELF

Thinking back
I can never be sure
whether I was great
at hide and seek

or just really unpopular

GOOGLE SEARCH INSPIRED POEM #1

I'm lost.
I'm lost where I am.
I'm lost for words.
I'm lost in French.
I'm lost in Spanish.
I'm lost in wonder.

I'm lost
without you.

SUPERKING-TAINTED WISDOM

NETWORK

I'm the permanent fixture
at the back of any room,
hovering in the space
where the movers and shakers aren't.

I'll be sipping complimentary wine,
pretending to check my phone,
a self-conscious phantom
shuffling, half smiling,
skilfully forgetting to
fill in the gaps of important conversations
which explode around me
in an incandescent glow of once-in-a-lifetime golden prospects.

Instead, my non-existent business cards will be thrown to the wind

and I'll inch away from the influential,
step lightly over serendipity,
fall through the cracks of every chance,

and I'll continue to make the most
of all those not-working opportunities.

PACKING

The case lay open on the backroom bed.
He'd only one more thing to pack.

But what with the scholarship,
his grinning face in the local gazette
and the acceptance letter, neatly ironed,
framed by his mam on the mantelpiece,

he'd put it out of his mind.
His background had become just that:

a stranger in the distance,
trying not to scuff its shoes
on the kerbstones of ambition.

But, like the spit on a grazed knee
on a rain dirt Sunday,
or the baked bean dinners and the ten-penny mixes,
or the jam on the Yorkshires
and Dad's alehouse apology chips,

it would always be there, always be his.

As snug as the fire-warmed towel on bath night,
as cold and stubborn as an outside bog.

How could he put that in a case?
How could he take it with him?

How could he even think of leaving it behind?

WAITING

It seemed like I was always waiting
for that donkey-jacketed figure
on the horizon,
lord of the slag heap
and the Labour club

tramping home from the Jug and Glass,
the week's graft smoothed away
with Brylcreem promise,
laden with chips and the freedom
of Friday, coalface thirst

slaked by alehouse divvy,
drinking through post-weekend
threats, the looming shadow
of the headstocks to come,
the taunting chink
of Monday's dawning motty disc.

And we would watch the late-night
horror double bills together,
him doing Boris Karloff impressions,
shuffling through the kitchen with
his pit boots on.

And Saturday was *Grandstand* and
chucked betting slips,
another hammering at the bar
and a cheap turn on the legion's stage
which blurred to next day's
roasting beef, his Mansfield
morning killer farts
accompanied by the waking rattle
of a never-ending Sunday cough.

And life would go on like that forever
until it nearly didn't when the
accident came instead.

And I remember walking
the long way to the hospital,
my older brother, gran and me,
through those woods where the
tree trunks, through my infant gaze,
became dinosaur feet sunk to ancient mud

till we reached the ward of those
broken men, industry-bled across
rows and rows of NHS beds,
my old man amongst them,

pit-black mascara round
those seen-it-all eyes,
legs crushed beneath
that white-sheeted box.

He was a big man
who'd never seemed so small.

And all I wanted was for him
to bundle me up in those arms
both soft as cushions and hard as bricks
to squeeze out all the fear from me.

And it took months
and he was healed
with faith and physio,
a handshake and a compo cheque

so they could cast him into that hole
again.

Where he stayed
and stayed
and stayed

till that sour time in the nineties when
I was older but no wiser, and our

connections fell away like that
five-thirty bastard morning cage,
leaving us searching in the dark
for things not to say, digging away
at each other's faults,

finding six of his, half a dozen of mine;
our stubbornness put us on different shifts.

And our conversations went to
chokedamp, suffocating black
till the bloody flecks in his handkerchief
became a tally of the years we'd never get back.

An overtime ban on your faltering health
where emphysema broke a heart
or two

and now I'm left staring at
that space on the horizon

where the headstocks and
that donkey-jacketed figure
once were.

And I'm still waiting

POTHOLES AND PARKING

is what it all comes down to.

All wondering whether the road ahead will be a bumpy one

and if there'll be a space for us
at the end of the journey

THE FUTURIST CINEMA

With a name like that it was
always tempting fate.

Knocked down now,
in its place a big wheel
to detract from recent
questioned votes and talk of dodgy
council bungs.

Seaside film reels switched
by the revolution for the business world.

Projections of a darker kind.

A spinning thing to hide the spin.

COMIC TIMING

Charlie Chaplin
was really poor as a kid.

If things hadn't turned out better
he might have become
a tramp.

YOU ARE EVERY EVERYTHING, I AM EVERY NOTHING

You are the ocean,
I am a drip.
You are a banquet,
I, a cold chip.

You are champagne,
I am Pepsi Max.
You are the internet,
I am Ceefax.

WHAT IS YOUR MUSIC?

Does your music deafen,
slam doors, threaten?
Is it a piano crashing to the busy street?
Is it the rick-a-ting-ting
of earphones which bleed
down the backs of seats
on a train trip
to hell?

Does your music flitter
like a petal on the breeze,
a throwaway moment on the
whim of a hit,
a catchy yet forgettable
spoonful of sugar,
a sweetie wrapper glimpsed
in the spilled bin of life?

Is your music scary,
a midnight score,
a drive-in horrific insomniac,
a zombie's fingers on a coffin lid,
an off-beat tapped
with bleached white bones,
a dreadnaught ghost
in a sea of dream?

Is your music weird,
quirky, bizarre,
Baby Jane makeup smeared across its face,
its rhythm a lingering lipstick kiss
on a bathroom mirror
in a house of love,
a tempo played
on the edge of time?

Is your music mournful,
quiet, lost, sipping its gin, getting drunk on itself
in those distant hours
of half-placed moons
where a lonely bow scrapes across
those strings of the night?

Does your music swing,
does your music move,
the dance across the moment
that keeps us all alive,
the soundtrack of the gym,
the sweat-stained suite,
the breathless beat against
the racetrack of the mind?

Is your music rooted
in a melody of soul?
Is it scrawled over a history
in a promise once made?
Is it freeform jazz?
Is it urban muse
or the subterranean
homesick blues?

Is your music wild,
possessed and raw,
a revolution rapping to
a symphony of hope,
the disco democratic
drummed into the heart,
a power ballad surging in
its infinite voice?

Is your music yours?
Is your music proud?
Does it come from the guts?
Is it hurricane-loud?
An orchestral manoeuvre

that lights up the dark?
Is it a piece that's been written?
Is it yet to played?

What is your music?
What is your music?

NO SOCIALIST GRACE

I turn up to the Socialism Now! meeting
dressed as Groucho, not Karl.
This doesn't go down too well.
Neither does the fact that
I don't know the words to 'The Red Flag',
so sing 'Lydia the Tattooed Lady',
instead, at the top of my voice.

This seems to upset
a peace-loving Trotskyist,
who, ironically, informs me that
he'd like to stave my head in

with an ice pick.

THIS AND THAT

HOME FRONT

Talks collapse,
tensions escalate and
insults drop like
missiles from the sky.

Negotiations fail again;
they retreat to opposite ends of the sofa,
leatherette between them,
a no-man's land,

coffee table neutral territory

where undrunk teacups barricade
the bomb site of their love.

TEA POEM

Fruit tea.
Tastes of neither.
Well done, hippies.

PHONE

I break my phone.
Can't fix it.
So start to wonder
how I ever thought I really owned it.

Realise it owns me.

Take it back to the shop.
Beg for mercy, renew
the Faustian contract doled out to me by
some tight-suit Herbert with sticky-up hair.

It's a cellular whiphand,
ensuring that I can never not be at work.

But I go along with it.
'Cause it tells me I am free.
Free to do what I can't.
Free to change everything.
Free to communicate,
my voice carried over
a thousand national thresholds.
When once I was ignored by the few
I am now ignored by the many.
Innumerate, dispassionate judgements in the aether.
Lack of interaction scrapes away at
this digital soul.

World reduced to two-inch screen,
this technology turns me not into promised bright star
but leaves me stumbling through the dark
with insufficient tiny torch,
trying not to make sense of it all.

But I'm terrified not to be part of this,
this wanting, needy necromancy,
this touchpad faux democracy
which is quick to tell me what I'm not,

the lowercase,
badly spelt furies
between the *you okay, hon?*s and bodiless hugs.

Hashtag love.
Hashtag hate.
Hashtag friend or enemy.
Hashtag me, me, me.

So I walk out of the shop with my phone.

I realise it owns me.
I'll never really own it.
I can't fix it.

I break my phone.

FEBRUARY 14TH

It will always be the day he died.
Not pink bows, trinkets or dinner surprise
but the brother's phone call set as rhyme,
the allotment keys left on the side.

The valentines drowned by condolence cards,
the neighbour's ghostly kind regards,
Davy lamp gone cold and dark.

His coronary every paper heart.

POOR SUNDAY

You shall not be missed. Can we
say that you were ever loved
aside from longer mornings
and stuffed blessed dinners? Did

anyone want you hanging round
after the football? Most knew
you could be cruel, but some
still clung on like you ever

made sense. Maybe I will see
you through the window sometime,
wave perhaps, or nod to you
on the street, help you carry

your Bible stories and car
boot sales into the hearse.
I will watch your boredom fade
again, into the winter,

but think of you in July.

STREET DANCE

Cue the music,
a grumble of midnight,
hailed down cabs.

Parting curtains are tarpaulin sheets
which flap on the scaffolding stage
cast in rust

where lamppost spotlights
pick out the lineup
of burned-out burlesquers
strutting their stuff
in pub kicking-out time,
half-learned routines.

Their fishnets are cracks
on pavement-grey legs,
their makeup the rain
which plasters the face,

their costume the night's
dwindling last-order sparkle,
the tattered remains of another
show done.

GETTING LOST

We come here to find ourselves
but mostly to get lost.

In this place, this space,
portal to the universe,
the beginning of a journey
into history's bookends
and futures unexplored.

Where hobbit holes
lead to wizard schools,
where Mills & Boon and
monsters meet in a Dewey
Decimal discovery
of well-thumbed wonder.

Where we can find recipes for
a better world, DIY our lives
back together, and dictators
are made to behave themselves
or be archived and put back on
the shelf.

We come here because it's free
yet its value is priceless.
No borders, backstops or hate speak here,
just free movement into an education
where bank accounts don't matter.

Council house or posh estate,
church, temple, mosque or chip shop, wherever we come from
we can all gather here
to worship in words
with this infinite congregation.

This community of superheroes,
time machines and aliens,

Shakespeare, celebrity,
psychology, philosophy,

where religion and science
might dance to the music
of jazz, folk or poetry.

We come here when words fail us
or when there is too much to say.
Where we can locate what we need to know
and everything they wish we couldn't.

Because when governments form not cabinets
but coffins for our ideas, our hopes, our art,

we still have this place,
where the books might be on loan
but what we gain from them is kept forever.

It's ours, this place.

This palace of knowledge,
this cathedral of classics,
this mansion of magic,
this shelter, this refuge
for the curious and stuck, the dreamers and the learners,
the weary and the excited

and this bleeding-heart poet,
who first came here when he was twelve
to escape from the cold outside and his parents' divorce
apocalypse
and instead found
Ray Bradbury, new worlds and rocket ships.

We still have this place.

This space, portal to the universe,
the beginning of a journey

into history's bookends
and futures unexplored.

Where hobbit holes
lead to wizard schools,
where Mills & Boon and
monsters meet in a Dewey
Decimal discovery
of well-thumbed wonder.

We come here to find ourselves
but mostly to get lost.

THIS AND THAT

It's always been this,
it's always been that.

From this sandstone cave that was dug with the bones,
carved with the stories of hooded thieves and rogues,

to this bridal boutique flogging Nottingham lace,
forming patterns of rebellion wedding attitude to place.

From that turgid river that will course through the veins,
this beer that slicks the throat, that match-day rain,

that kaleidoscope street that's alive with the glow
of this Windrush generation's cultural growth.

From that Sally Army march in a cold Christmas prayer
to this kiddie's feet splashing through fountains in the square.

From this foodbank to that bistro, this cup of mushy peas,
that ex-council house and this temporary beach.

From this pit boot worn through in the dust down below
to that click of pink heels in hen do's mid-flow.

From this library which helped me to reconnect the lines
between the confused history and more enlightened times

where that hidden love need be secret no more
in this rainbow-kissing Pride on a Hockley dawn.

From that Raleigh Chopper to this Uber cab,
to a city's heart crossed with tram-line tracks.

In a promise to move forward whilst acknowledging a past

it's always been this
and always been that.

MOVIEDROME

Alex,
be our portal,
trash cult guardian punk,
custodian of grindhouse love,
always.

PERFECTLY DAMAGED

His songs are wrecks,
godless and unsaved,
adrift in the dark,
abandoned moments,
angels lost.

His words are
unsmoked cigarettes,
each verse another
crumpled prayer,
each pause a deep eternity,
threatened by sin,
kissed by indifference.

His voice is cavernous,
deluded and sincere,
a gloomy miracle to behold
in the rain of this Saturday cold
reminding us we are dead no more.

Lazarus returns
to the Labour club.

PAZ

Saw Paz today.

Not seen him
since we were kids.

He was at the bus stop
near Tesco. Fag-orange fingers gripping plaggy bag as if the
bitter wind might blow
the weekly shop or his tenuous sense of being away.

Always the big lad at
school. My mate, protector.
We were drawn closer by our love of AC/DC, our outcast status
and crappy pov trainers. We stood
about the edges on the brink of hesitant glories, unacknowledged
cogs in the machinery of comprehensive schooling.

Now, he'd never looked so small.
His face a mess of lines cut too deep, skin a betrayal,
market cheap and out of date, reality-bitten,
a bargain unbought.

His gaze a dissembled action,
searching for a meaning between
the hurried cold pedestrians
and rain-slashed cars.

Searching for a place before that day back then
when that new teacher came.

'Cause he might have been a big lad, but he was still only a lad.

And the teacher was a bloke who should've known better.

Should have been prosecuted.
Should never have been allowed to just leave town like that.

Leaving Paz with nowhere else to go,
no matter how far his shitty trainers took him.

He didn't see me.
Like we all stopped seeing him at school after that day.

I could've talked.
Said *ey up*.
I didn't.
I couldn't.

I saw Paz today.

DREAMIN'

She just decided she was going to fly.

Instead of arguing with gravity
she simply renegotiated her contract with the ground.

Chose to fall up,
not down.

ACKNOWLEDGEMENTS

Thanks to Bob Dylan and his freak show, troubadour kaleidoscope blues. Thanks to Ray Bradbury for his Martian-chronicling stargazed truths. Thanks to Peter Cushing and his Frankenstein maniacal Hammer film screams. Thanks to Carnival of Souls and its Salt Lake psychedelic death cult dreams. Thanks to Allen Ginsberg and his sweet catastrophic electric psalms. Thanks to William Burroughs and the creeped-out poetry in his trackmarked arms. Thanks to Alice Cooper and his ragdoll, theatrical, guillotine drag. Thanks to Bette Davis and her Baby Jane bitchfest camp-as-hell hag.

Lightning Source UK Ltd.
Milton Keynes UK
UKHW011601140821
388862UK00004B/56